better together*

*This book is best read together, grownup and kid.

 akidsco.com

a kids
book
about

a kids book about

BLOCKCHAIN

by Harold Hughes

A Kids Co.
Editor Jennifer Goldstein
Designer Gabby Nguyen
Creative Director Rick DeLucco
Studio Manager Kenya Feldes
Sales Director Melanie Wilkins
Head of Books Jennifer Goldstein
CEO and Founder Jelani Memory

DK
Senior Production Editor Jennifer Murray
Senior Production Controller Louise Minihane
Senior Acquisitions Editor Katy Flint
Acquisitions Project Editor Sara Forster
Managing Art Editor Vicky Short
Managing Director, Licensing Mark Searle

First American edition, 2025
Published in the United States by DK Publishing, 1745 Broadway, 20th Floor,
New York, NY 10019

First published in Great Britain in 2025 by
Dorling Kindersley Limited, 20 Vauxhall Bridge Road, London SW1V 2SA
A Penguin Random House Company

The authorised representative in the EEA is
Dorling Kindersley Verlag GmbH. Arnulfstr. 124, 80636 Munich, Germany

A catalog record for this book is available from the Library of Congress.
A CIP catalogue record for this book is available from the British Library.
ISBN: 978-0-2417-4314-0

DK books are available at special discounts when purchased in bulk for sales
promotions, premiums, fund-raising, or education use. For details, contact:
DK Publishing Special Markets, 1745 Broadway, 20th Floor, New York, NY 10019
SpecialSales@dk.com

Printed and bound in China
www.dk.com
akidsco.com

MIX
Paper | Supporting
responsible forestry
FSC™ C018179

This book was made with Forest
Stewardship Council™ certified
paper – one small step in DK's
commitment to a sustainable future.
Learn more at **www.dk.com/uk/
information/sustainability**

To my "Little Leos",
Carter and Camryn,
and my non-fungible dad.

Intro
for grownups

As grownups, there are 3 magic words we can use to explore ideas that can change us forever. **I. Don't. Know.**

The phrase "I don't know" can unlock vital information, erase expectations, and create opportunities to learn new things. When we use that magic phrase with our kids, it allows us to put ourselves in their shoes and work to arrive at an answer through their lens. That is what I set out to do with this book about blockchain.

My goal for this book is not to have all of the answers but rather to give examples of how blockchain technology can—and will—be used in our lives and the lives of our kids. Blockchain is fundamental to many new applications that we may hear about on a daily basis. From NFTs (non-fungible tokens) to the metaverse, more and more cases for the use of blockchain are being created.

This book was written to help start conversations around this revolutionary technology and create opportunities for grownups and kids to explore how blockchain has the potential to enhance and improve many aspects of our lives.

What if I
told you that
BLOCK

CHAIN

is the technology
of the future?

That someday, you'll use it everywhere?

When you
go to school.

When you
play your favorite video game.

When you
buy something.

And even when you
make art!

You probably don't know what blockchain is yet, but that's **OK**—I promise.

Because guess what?
A lot of grownups don't know
what blockchain is yet either!

The cool thing is that
by the end of this book,
both you and your grownup
will know more about
this new and exciting
<u>technology</u>* called blockchain.

*We'll cover lots of terms in this book. Each time you
see an underlined word (like <u>technology</u>), you'll know you can
find out more about it at the end of the book.

And maybe, just maybe, you'll have some ideas about how you can

change the world with it.

So you might be asking yourself, what is blockchain?

Let me explain.

Blockchain is

a new and different way to store or keep data.

Now I want you to think about where you store your things.

You probably put your clothes

Your dishes go

Your books go

in a closet.

in a cupboard.

in a backpack
or on a bookshelf.

But when it comes to data, you store it in a

data

base.

I know all this talk about data can sound kind of boring.

But that couldn't be further from the truth.

Because when we talk about data and blockchain, things get **really** interesting.

You see,
blockchain is an amazing
new kind of <u>database.</u>

It is more

fair and <u>transparent</u>

than other types of databases.

Older databases are often controlled by one person or company, meaning they are <u>centralized</u>.

But blockchain databases are

decentralized,

which means they're controlled by many people or companies.

Did you know that a blockchain database allows anyone in the world, ANYONE, to see inside it in order to call out problems and keep things fair?

And another cool thing about blockchain is that nothing is deleted.

Ever!

Every time new information is added to the database, a new data block is created.

That's why it's called blockchain.

That new block is then added to the previous blocks (that's where the **"chain"** part of the word comes from).

ALL OF THE DATA IS
CONNE

As the chain gets longer, more information is stored and connected.

And guess what?!

It's ALL public, which makes it nearly impossible to cheat.

Why?

Because it isn't a secret!

OK, OK, OK...this is cool and all, but still kind of complicated, right?

Let's talk about some
of the ways blockchain
is being used today!

Did you know

musicians

are using blockchain
to sell their songs so
their fans can own them?

With blockchain,
fans are able to
not only play the song,
but also get money
when the song is played.

Did you know

artists

are using blockchain
to sell their art?

With blockchain,
the artist can make a rule
—using a <u>smart contract</u>—
that they get paid for every sale
of each piece of their artwork.
(That means every time the
piece of art changes hands.)

Did you know some countries are already using

cryptocurrency

as one of their official forms of money?

With blockchain, <u>digital</u> money and assets (called cryptocurrencies), can be created and used just like paper money or coins.

Why does all of this matter?

Why should anyone
use blockchain today?

Because...

blockchain is transparent.

Each transaction is visible to everyone.

Blockchain promotes trust.

There is less room to cheat the system.

Blockchain is decentralized.

There isn't only one person who knows the rules.

Now let's dream up what the future could look like with ―――

blockchain.

In the future, maybe more of us will buy things using blockchain with cryptocurrencies like Bitcoin or Ethereum.

This could help the

1.7 billion people

around the world who
don't have access to a bank.

In the future,

maybe **ALL** of us will <u>vote</u> in elections with blockchain.

Imagine seeing your vote count on the blockchain and seeing <u>democracy</u> in action.

In the future,

maybe the video games you play will use blockchain to build your character.

That way you can take
that character into
any game you want.

In the future,

you'll think of new and amazing ways to use blockchain to...

create, make, build, and discover.

BUT WHY WAIT?

Outro
for grownups

Whew! We did it! If you're reading this page, you made it to the end of *A Kids Book About Blockchain*, and at the very least, you will now be able to better navigate those holiday dinners where people talk about <u>crypto</u>.

Hopefully this book has helped you move from "I don't know" to "Tell me more" as you and your kid embark on this new and exciting adventure. As you further explore ways to use blockchain technology, remember that while this technology may be new to grownups, our kids are growing up in a digital era where its uses are more common. Whether you decide to dive into NFTs or venture out into the metaverse, be sure to take those next steps with discernment and an open mind.

Words To Know

Bitcoin: A digital currency that can be exchanged between people without the need for a bank.

Centralized: To concentrate power and authority in a single central organization.

Cryptocurrency (or crypto): A digital asset that is given value and used in exchange for goods or services.

Data: Information about all sorts of stuff that is sometimes saved in digital form.

Database: A collection of data that can be searched by using a computer.

Decentralized: Sharing the control of an action or organization among multiple people.

Democracy: A government in which the people vote to elect their representatives at routinely-held free elections.

Digital: Something you can access only by using an electronic device, like a computer or smartphone.

Ethereum: A program that uses smart contracts to ensure that the cryptocurrency, Ether, is used fairly.

Metaverse: A network of interconnected virtual worlds.

NFTs: Non-fungible tokens (or NFTs) are unique digital assets that cannot be duplicated. Fungible means the opposite and refers to assets which can be used interchangeably, such as dollar bills.

For example, if something costs 5 dollars, you could use any $5 bill to pay for it—each dollar bill is interchangeable for another dollar bill, which isn't true of NFTs.

Smart Contract: A set of rules which outline what a system does every time new information is added.

Technology: The use of knowledge in a particular area to create, solve problems, or accomplish a task.

Transparent: When something is shared and none of the details about it are hidden.

Vote: To share your opinion about something in order to help a group make an important decision.

Made to empower.

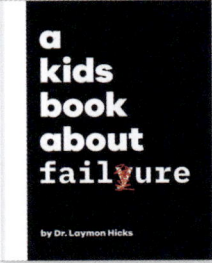

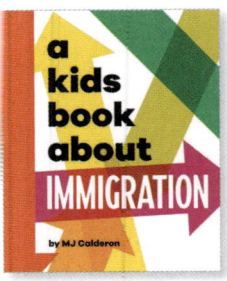

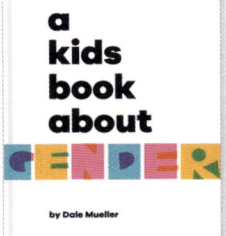
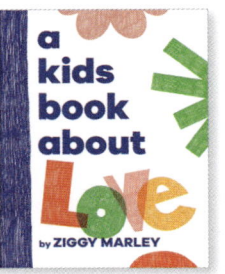

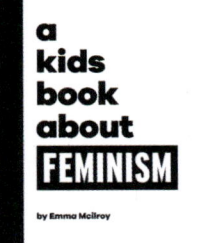

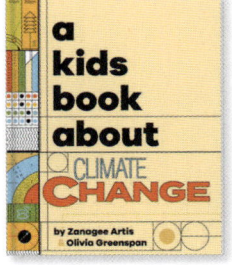

Discover more at akidsco.com